JOKES
GIGGLES
& GUFFAWS

JOKES GIGGLES & GUFFAWS

Selected by HELEN HOKE
Pictures by HARO

Franklin Watts, Inc., New York, 1975

Originally published by Franklin Watts Limited, London,
under the title of Jokes, Jokes, Jokes 2

Copyright © 1973 by Franklin Watts Limited
Copyright © 1975 by Helen Hoke

Library of Congress Catalog Card Number: 75-6047
ISBN 0-531-02844-5

Printed in the United States of America
6 5 4 3 2 1

CONTENTS

ABOUT THIS BOOK

Do you know *what* makes people laugh? Why they keel over hysterically at one joke and remain stone-faced throughout another? Why one riddle tickles their fancy and another leaves them quite, quite cold? If you do, I wish you'd let me know, because after writing seven joke books I'm still not 100% sure.

The thing is people have such extraordinary, unfathomable senses of humour. And they all seem to be as individual as finger-prints. I once watched a sober-suited, rather elderly and frightening gentleman laugh until the tears dripped down his waistcoat, at two clowns on television throwing custard pies at each other.

But that's a schoolboy joke, I thought to myself. What on earth does he find so funny? So I asked him.

7

And he said that when he was a small boy, he'd been taken to the circus and during a pie-throwing contest in the ring, one had whizzed through the air and landed smack! in his face. It got in his hair, it got in his eyes, it even went right down his neck. He had left the circus ignominiously, in tears. But now it was happening to someone else—and that was *so* much funnier!

The thing is you never really know just what special thing it is that's making people laugh. The joke itself, or a triggered-off memory of their own. That's why I now tell each joke that I am considering for one of my joke books to at least five people first. If three people giggle or even crack their faces just a little, the joke goes IN. If only two people out of five laugh, then the joke goes OUT. I've learned to work on the principle that what makes most people laugh *is* the funniest, otherwise I'd go bananas trying to sort out all their *private* reasons. (Now what was it that my dentist *really* thought was so very, very funny about that joke about false teeth! Etc. Etc.)

(Do please laugh!)

Helen Hoke

ABSOLUTELY AWFUL

●

EDUCATED EDDIE, *bird-watching*: Oh, look! There's a yellow-breasted gulp.

FRIEND: What's a gulp?

EDUCATED EDDIE: Well, it's somewhat like a swallow, but noisier.

CRITICAL CURTIS, *to his friend as they were paddling in the sea*: Gosh, aren't your feet dirty!

DUMB BUNNY: Well, we didn't have a holiday last year.

•

Discontented Dolly complains that the walls of her room are so thin, you can hear people in the next room changing their minds.

•

What can you hold in your left hand that you can't hold in your right hand?

Your right elbow.

•

VISITING FRIEND: I see you have tomatoes growing in your garden—tell me—why are some of them so poorly developed?

EDUCATED EDDIE: Well, those are ketchup tomatoes. They start off slowly, but they ketchup by late spring.

•

A miserly farmer of Nenagh,
Grew daily more leanagh and leanagh.
    He remained undistressed,
    Though his back touched his chest,
For the money he saved made him meanagh.

10

JERRY: What is a hippopotamus after it is five years old?

PERRY: Six years old.

Critical Cathy tells of a very poor couple she knows: they had been married three whole weeks and the bride still made the morning tea in her nightdress. They couldn't afford a tea-pot.

MOTHER (*teaching her son arithmetic*): Now take the Smith family—there's Mummy, Daddy and the baby. How many does that make?

BRIGHT SON: Two and one to carry.

•

JOHNNIE: My parrot can't talk.

LONNIE: Really?

JOHNNIE: Yes, I asked him what is three minus three and he said nothing.

•

JILL: What makes men mean?

BILL: The letter A.

•

RAFE Where do you find the most lamb?

LAFE: Between the head and the tail.

•

MAC: What did Little John say when Robin Hood fired at him?

JACK: That was an arrow escape.

•

GROGGY: What is the definition of a mermaid?

FOGGY: A deep she-fish.

•

Why is an elephant an unwelcome guest?

Because he has to bring his trunk along.

•

The local weather forecaster for a popular south coast resort was wrong so often that it became a standing joke. Should he predict rain, everybody came out to swim and sunbathe. And if he swore it would be sunny, they made plans to go to the pictures.

After a while the hopeless forecaster asked
for a transfer to another area.

"What's your reason for wanting to leave?"
asked his boss.

"The climate doesn't agree with me."

●

Alphabet Puzzle

1. What letter is something you see with?

    I *(aɪ)*

2. What letter is a large body of water?

    C *(see)*

3. What letter asks a question?

    Y *(why)*

ιt letter is a talkative bird?

J (ɡʌʊ)

What letter is a buzzing insect?

B (əəq)

6. What letter is yourself?

I

7. What letter is the person you speak to?

U (noɷ)

8. What letter belongs here: I am; we —?

R (əɪʊ)

9. What letter is an oriental man's pigtail?

Q (ənənb)

10. What letter means one of anything?

A

11. What letter is an exclamation?

O (¡ɥo)

12. What letter is a vegetable?

P (vəɋ)

13. What letter is a hot drink?

T (vəɿ)

14. What letter is a printer's measure?

M (uɿə)

BLISSFULLY BATTY

There was an old man of Key West
Who had numerous spots on his vest.
   He said: "I don't think
   That many were ink,
But those that were wine are the best."

● A hunter who potted two toucans
Said, "Now I will put them in two cans."
　　Said two canners who heard:
　　"It's a rather large bird—
You can't can two toucans in two cans."

● What should you do if you split your sides laughing?

Run fast until you get a stitch in them.

● SHOPPER: Baker! Have you any pies left?
BAKER:　Yes, madam.
SHOPPER: Well, you shouldn't have baked so many!

● JERRY: Why did the little boy put his car on the stove?
PERRY: He wanted a hot rod.

●　　Young Peter, son of a Cape Kennedy missiles engineer, was in kindergarten for the first time.
　　When the teacher announced that the children were going to learn to count, the boy said proudly that he already knew how, and he started to demonstrate:
　　"10-9-8-7-6-5-4-3-2-1-Nuts!"

BARBER: Do you want your beard trimmed?

HIPPIE: Nope, jus' cut a hole in it.

BARBER: What for?

HIPPIE: My bird wants to see the tie she gave me for Christmas.

HOLIDAY GUEST, *on a farm*: Mr. Robbins, I enjoy this place so much—the food is good, the air fresh, I sleep well. There is just one thing: two or three times a day, that old sow keeps coming into my room . . . Do you think she's taken a fancy to me *(he added, laughing.)*

MR. ROBBINS: Well, no—not that. *(He leaned over confidentially and explained)*, that's her room, winter-times.

CRITICAL CAL: Want to lose ten pounds of ugly fat?

ADIPOSE AL: Sure.

CRITICAL CAL: Cut off your head.

One Halloween night Mrs. Goodneighbour answered her doorbell and there stood a tiny little girl dressed in a skeleton costume, but wearing no mask.

Mrs. Goodneighbour asked her, "Why don't you wear your mask?"

A tiny voice whispered, "I'm scared of it."

What are the finest animals on earth?

Ground mice.

● Boss: How come you're only carrying one sack, when the other men are carrying two?

Workman: Well, I suppose they're too lazy to make two trips, the way I do.

● Farmer: My eldest boy works as a New York City bootblack, and he's making a fortune.

Clever Barmaid: Oh. I see ... you make hay while the son shines?

●

SAVING SAM, *to his friend*: Well, what do you know!
I just read in the newspaper how you can make
your money go farther!

SPENDTHRIFT SPIRO: Gee! How?

SAVING SAM: It says here, "Send £5 to Box 1280,
Grand Central Post Office, Dupetown.

COMPLETELY CORNY

• What is the hardest thing about learning to skate?

The ice.

•

Why is it useless to send a telegram to Washington
today?

Because he is dead.

•

KENNY: What coat has no buttons and must be put
on wet?
LENNY: A coat of paint.

•

SMART: What is the difference between an oak tree
and a tight boot.
ALEC: One makes acorns and the other makes
corns ache.

•

TESS: Name a band in which there are no musical
instruments?
BESS: An elastic band.

•

ARTY: Why did the man who walked three miles
not get very far?
SMARTY: He only moved two feet.

•

A very fat lady was lying on the beach
when a life-guard asked her to move up onto the
promenade.

"Why?" she asked indignantly.

"Because the tide wants to come in."

22

Mary had a little lamb.
It had a sooty foot.
And into Mary's bread and jam
Its sooty foot it put.

An old couple went on a long-looked-forward-to holiday, which ended in a ship-wreck.

They were the only survivors.

By the end of a few weeks on a desert island their clothes were in rags and all the food they had been able to rescue from the ship-wreck was gone. They were in despair!

"Oh, my!" sighed the wife. "Things just couldn't be worse!"

"Oh yes, they could!" her husband answered. "I might have bought return tickets!"

THERE WAS A LITTLE GIRL

There was a little girl,
And she had a little curl
   Right in the middle of her forehead.
When she was good
She was very, very good,
   And when she was bad she was horrid!

One day she went upstairs,
When her parents, unawares,
    In the kitchen were occupied with meals
And she stood upon her head
In her little trundle-bed,
    And then began hooraying with her heels.

Her mother heard the noise,
And she thought it was the boys
    A-playing at a combat in the attic;
But when she climbed the stair,
And found Jemima there,
She took and she did spank her most emphatic!
                                        Anonymous

DELIGHTFULLY DOPEY

●

WILLIE: Ma, if the baby was to eat tadpoles, would it give him a big bass voice like a frog?
MOTHER: Good gracious, no! They'd kill him.
WILLIE: Well, they didn't!

•

An aging lady started to go bald, so she went to the chemist for a hair restorer.

"Do you want this little bottle or this tall one?" asked the chemist.

"Make it the small bottle," she told him. "I don't care for long hair."

•

DOPEY: Why do people always put their right shoe on first?

SMARTY: It would be foolish to put the wrong shoe on first.

•

What do you have if there are two ducks and a cow?

Quackers and milk.

•

What would you have if your lawn mower ran over a bird?

Shredded tweet.

•

Why doesn't a bike stand up by itself?

Because it's two-tired.

•

What is the best day to fry?

Friday.

•

CUTE KENNY: What made the lobster blush?

CLEVER KATE: It saw the salad dressing.

●

MOPE: My aunt collects fleas for a living.
DOPE: What does your uncle do?
MOPE: Scratches himself.

●

    A tourist was furious with the tough steak he had been served.

    "Waiter," he shouted, "get me the manager. I can't eat this steak!"

    "It's no use calling *him*, sir. He can't eat it either. He's on a diet."

DOPEY DAN: *phoning the fire service*: Fire! Fire! Come quick!

FIREMAN: Where is it?

DOPEY DAN: In my house.

FIREMAN: I mean the *location* of the fire.

DOPEY DAN: My kitchen!

Dopey Dan says that why he prefers to sit in the rear seat of the last row in the classroom is because, sitting there, he gets last chance at a question. By then it's almost impossible for him to guess wrong.

"Papa, are you growing taller all the time?"

"No, son. Why do you ask?"

"'Cause the top of your head is poking up through your hair."

•

Romantic Rena, explaining why she bought a gorgeous new tulle evening dress, said, "You've got to be a little different if you want to get noticed. After all, would anyone give the Tower of Pisa a second glance if it were standing up straight?"

•

Little Jane asked her teacher, as the children were leaving for home, "Please, Miss Mitchell, tell me—what did I learn in school today? My daddy always wants to know."

•

DORA: When does a man become two men?
NORA: When he is beside himself.

•

SMARTY: What! Out on a day like this—it's below freezing! You'll catch a cold.
DOPEY: Oh, no! Selling papers keeps up the circulation.

•

VICAR: Do you say your prayers every night, Bobby?
BOBBY: Oh, no! Some nights I don't want anything.

•

JASON: What is black and white and red all over?
MASON: A sunburned zebra.

30

"I want our Sammy to be a philanthropist when he grows up," said Mama.

"Why do you want Sammy to be that?" asked Papa.

"All the philanthropists you read about are millionaires."

●

"Was Papa the first man who ever proposed to you, Mama?"

"Yes, but why do you ask?"

"I was just thinking that you might have done better if you had shopped around a little more."

●

POLICEMAN, *to lost little girl*: What name does your mother call your father?

LOST LITTLE GIRL, *shocked*: Oh, my! She doesn't call him names, she *likes* him!

●

JOY: Why should a savage dog always be a hungry man's best friend?

LOY: Because he's sure to give him a bite.

HOW TO TELL BAD NEWS

(No News, or What Killed the Dog)

MR. H., *to his hired man, on returning from a long business trip abroad*: Ha! George, old boy—how are you? How are things at home?

GEORGE: Not good, sir; your dog died.

MR. H.: Poor Mag! So he's gone. How came he to die?

GEORGE: Overeat himself, sir.

MR. H.: *Did* he? A greedy dog; why? What did he get he liked so well?

GEORGE: Horseflesh, sir; he died of eating horse-flesh.

MR. H.: How came he to get so much horseflesh?

GEORGE: All your father's horses, sir.

MR. H.: What! Are *they* dead, too?

GEORGE: Ay, sir; they died of overwork.

MR. H.: And why were they overworked, pray?

GEORGE: To carry water, sir.

MR. H.: To carry water! and what were they carrying water for?

GEORGE: Sure, sir, to put out the fire.

MR. H.: Fire! *what* fire?

GEORGE: O, sir, your father's house is burned to the ground.

MR. H.: My father's house burned down! And how came it to be set on fire?

GEORGE: I think, sir, it must have been the torches.

MR. H.: Torches! *what* torches?

GEORGE: At your mother's funeral.

MR. H.: My mother *dead*!

GEORGE: Ah, poor lady! she never looked up, after it happened.

MR. H.: After *what* happened?

GEORGE: The loss of your father.

MR. H.: My *father* gone, too?

GEORGE: Yes, poor gentleman! he took to his bed as soon as he heard of it.

MR. H.: Heard of *what*?

GEORGE: The bad news, sir, and please your honour.

MR. H.: What! *more* miseries! *more* bad news!

GEORGE: Yes, sir; your bank has failed, and your credit is gone, and you are not worth a shilling in the world. I made bold, sir, to meet you at the train, for I thought you would like to hear the news as quickly as possible.

ANONYMOUS

33

EFFUSIVELY EFFERVESCENT

●

"It's not true that I married a millionaire," said Cynthia to a friend after a few months of marriage. "I *made* him one."

"What was he before you married him?" asked the friend.

Cynthia answered, "A multi-millionaire."

The camp medical officer was driving out to town in his car when the vehicle stalled just outside the canteen. A crowd of onlookers soon gathered, with smiles on their faces, and one of them said, "What's the matter, sir—won't it go?"

"Of course it won't go," said the officer. "Do any of you have any suggestions?"

"Yes," said another voice. "Give it an aspirin and mark it 'Fit for duty'!"

An orderly officer was inspecting the cook-house before the evening meal. He thought he would test the intelligence of the cook on duty.

"Why is it," he asked, pointing to the hot water in the large pot, "that the water is only boiling around the edges of that pot, and not in the middle?"

The cook said, "Ah! well, you see, sir, the water around the edges is for the guards' tea; they come in an hour before the others."

SOUR SUE says that all ladies' hats are different— because milliners rarely make the same mistake twice.

A man stopped by the veterinarian's to bring back the family puppy who was being treated there. When he reached home he told his wife, "Jerry cannot have enjoyed his visit to the vet, he barked all the way home as if he was trying to tell me something."

"No wonder," said his wife. "He was trying to tell you that you brought the wrong dog home."

ADDLEPATED AL knows a boy scout who did so many good turns that he felt dizzy!

FERVENTLY

FOOLISH

Lord Egbert, *ailing*: Did you cancel all my engagements, as I told you, Batterson?

Valet: Yes, sir, but Lady Ermyntrude didn't take it very well. She said you were supposed to marry her next Monday!

Little Tommy watched his mother sprinkling flour over a piece of fish before frying it.

The next morning he saw her sprinkling talcum powder over his new baby brother at bathtime.

"I can tell you before you start, Mummy," he said, "you'll need a bigger frying pan for him."

The master, to impress on his pupils the need of thinking before speaking, told them to count fifty before saying anything important, and one hundred if it was *very* important.

Next day he was speaking, standing with his back to the fire, when he noticed several lips moving rapidly.

Suddenly the whole class shouted: "Ninety-eight, ninety-nine, a hundred. Your coat's on fire, sir."

A husband returned home from work one evening to find his wife painting the livingroom walls furiously, paint flying everywhere.

"Whatever are you doing, rushing like that! Why don't you do it more slowly and carefully?"

"Well, you see," said his harried little bride, pushing her hair out of her eyes," I don't have much paint, and I'm trying to finish the walls before it runs out."

An old gentleman, clad in a somewhat youthful suit of light grey flannel, sat on a bench in the park enjoying the spring day.

"What's the matter, sonny?" he asked a small boy who lay on the grass and stared at him intently. "Why don't you go and play?"

"Don't want to," the boy replied.

"But it is not natural," the old gentleman insisted, "for a boy to be so quiet. *Why* don't you want to?"

"Oh, I'm waiting," the little fellow answered. "I'm just waiting till you get up . . . A man painted that bench about fifteen minutes ago."

Little Paul was sitting with his mother in church during the wedding of her eldest daughter. Halfway through the service, he noticed that his mother was crying.

"Why are you crying, Mother?" he asked. "It's not *your* wedding."

Granny took Harry to his first concert. The conductor was leading the orchestra and directing the soprano soloist as well. Harry was fascinated.

"Granny, why is that man shaking his stick at that lady?" he asked.

"Hush! He's not shaking his stick at her."

"Then what is she screaming for?"

A man returned home after his first holiday abroad and he didn't look very happy.

"Did you enjoy yourself?" asked his neighbour.

"Well, to tell you the truth, I'm so glad to be home I'm not sorry I went."

SLEEPY MAN, *answering the telephone at 4.00 a.m.*: Hello . . .

CALLER: What number is this?

SLEEPY MAN: Well, *you* ought to know—*you* dialled it!

A pretty young lady driver went into a police station, and handed the desk sergeant a parking ticket.

"Did one of your men lose this?" she asked. "I found it on my windshield."

PROFESSOR: Er—dear, what's the meaning of these flowers on my desk today?

WIFE: Meaning? Why, it's your wedding anniversary.

PROFESSOR: Is that so? Well, well, do let me know when yours is so I may do the same for you.

CLEO: I'm glad I wasn't born in Italy.

LEO: Why?

CLEO: Because I can't speak a word of Italian.

MOTHER: Frankie, it's time you were up. The birds were all up long ago.

FRANKIE (*drowsily*): Well, if I had to sleep in a nest of sticks and straws, I'd get up early, too.

TERRY: How old are you?

OLD JIM: Well, I'd be eighty-seven in June, except for one thing.

TERRY: What's that?

OLD JIM: I were born in October.

A woman came to an appointment with a psychiatrist, leading a hippopotamus.

"I'm so worried about my husband, doctor," she said. "He keeps thinking he's a hippopotamus!"

A very old and feeble fellow had been found guilty of an offence and, as he was an habitual offender, he was given a stiff sentence.

"I'll never live to do it," said the old man.

"Never mind," said the judge gently, patting him on the shoulder, "you just do what you can"

●

PORTER: This train goes to Newcastle and points north.

OLD LADY: Well, I want one that goes to York, and I don't care *which* way it points.

●

An elderly lady, after long trips through impressive hallways and an hour of waiting, was permitted to see a high-up assistant in the Department of Agriculture.

"But I want to see the Minister of Agriculture himself," she protested.

"He's not in just now, madam," said the official. "Can't you tell me what it is you want to see him about?"

"Well, I have a geranium that isn't doing so well . . ."

Grandmother Sutherland didn't like changes of any sort, and the new dial phone was no exception. "But just what don't you like about it, Grandma?" someone asked.

"Suppose I get the wrong number," replied Grandma. "Who can I blame it on?"

The old man was in his last illness and there seemed no point in keeping the truth about his condition from him any longer.

"You're a very sick man," the doctor told him. "I'm sure you would want to know straight facts. Now, is there anyone you would like to see?"

Feebly the patient nodded his head. "Yes," he said, almost inaudibly, "I'd like to see another doctor."

HILARIOUSLY HORRIFIC

An angler, trying to land a big fish, fell off the end of the pier.

"I can't swim," he shouted, "I can't swim!"

A drunk, walking along the promenade, heard him and called back, "So what? I can't play the piano, but I'm not shouting about it."

●

A lazy man was fishing off the end of the pier when an onlooker fell into the sea. It quickly became obvious that he couldn't swim, but the fisherman did nothing except to say as the man came up for the second time, "When you go down again, will you see if my bait is still on the hook?"

●

A wealthy playboy bought an expensive diving-suit and helmet and waded out into the sea. Walking about on the ocean bed, he was surprised to see a swimmer flailing about in nothing but a pair of swimming-trunks.

Extracting a special notebook from one of the pockets of his diving-suit, the playboy wrote,

"What are you doing down here without a diving-suit and helmet?"

The man snatched the notebook and wrote, "Drowning."

●

For many centuries it used to be the custom in North Africa for women to walk behind their menfolk. Since World War II, however, they have walked a few paces ahead of them. There are still, you see, lots of unexploded mines about.

A ghost in the town of Macroom,
One night found a ghoul in his room.
  They argued all night,
  As to which had the right,
To frighten the wits out of whom.

A cute curate who lived in Dundalk,
Proclaimed he could fly like a hawk,
　　Cheered by thousands of people,
　　He leaped from a steeple,
But the splash-down proved it just talk.

The pilot of an army reconnaissance plane persuaded his friend to come up for a spin one Saturday afternoon. Showing off, the pilot put the plane into a steep dive, only pulling out at the last moment, some 50 feet from the ground.

"Did you see them scatter?" he yelled to his companion. "Half of them down there thought we were going to have an accident!"

"Half of them up here thought so, too!" gasped his friend.

Humpty Dumpty sat on a wall,
Humpty Dumpty had a great fall;
All the King's horses and all the King's men
Had scrambled eggs.

VISITOR: I see there's a stuffed lion's head in your uncle's den.

GEORGIE: Yes, my uncle Benjy spent several years in the jungle, hunting for a lion.

VISITOR: What is it stuffed *with*?

GEORGIE: My uncle Benjy. He finally found one.

A big game hunter in South Africa heard a terrible scream from his friend ahead of him in the jungle.

"What's the matter?" he shouted.

"A lion has bitten off my foot," came the agonised reply.

"Which one?"

"How should *I* know? All these lions look alike to me."

A patient, who was coming round from the anaesthetic in the ward after an operation, exclaimed audibly:

"Thank goodness! That's over!"

"Don't be too sure," said the patient in the next bed. "They left a sponge in me and had to cut me open again."

Just then the surgeon who had performed the operation stuck his head in the door and called out:

"Has anybody seen my hat?"

MR. GRADY: Sorry, old man, my hen got out and scratched up your garden.

MR. BRADY: Oh, that's all right, my dog ate your hen.

MR. GRADY: Fine! I just ran over your dog and killed him.

Algy met a bear,
Soon the bear was bulgy,
And the bulge was Algy.

A horrified mother got on the telephone to her doctor. "Doctor, doctor! What shall I do! I found my baby in his sandbox, eating handfuls of sand!"

The doctor asked the weeping mother what had she already done. When she told him she had given the baby several glasses of water, he said that was the best thing she could have done. The poor woman was still nervous about it, and asked what else could she possibly do.

"Nothing else," he said, adding, "Just don't give him any cement."

MISSIONARY: Why are you looking at me that way?
CANNIBAL: I'm a food inspector.

JILL: What is the difference between a dressmaker
   and a nurse?
TILL: One cuts the dresses, while the other dresses
   the cuts.

A missionary was captured by cannibals, tied up and thrown into a huge kettle to cook, when the chief appeared and began to talk to him in perfect English. The chief explained his splendid diction and vocabulary by saying that he'd gone to Oxford.

"You're an Oxford man," said the missionary. "And you *still* eat your fellow man?"

"Yes," replied the chief. "But now I use a knife and fork."

IN CRED IBLY IDIOTIC

AUNT AGNES: Well, Eliza, were you very brave at the dentist's?

ELIZA: Yes, Auntie, I was.

AUNT AGNES: Then here's the money I promised you. And now tell me what he did to you.

ELIZA: He pulled out two of brother Bertie's teeth!

53

JOAN: What do the angels do in heaven, Mummy?
MOTHER: They sing and play harps.
JOAN: Don't they have any radios?

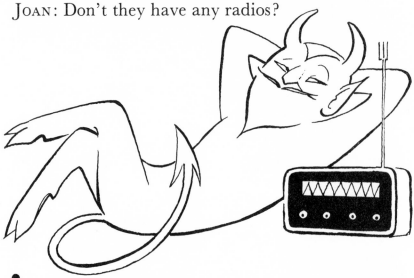

Towards the end of the last war, the chauffeur to the Chief of Staff was continually being asked by his fellow-soldiers if he'd heard any news about when the war was going to end. He promised to tell them the minute he had anything to report.

One day he came into the mess-hall and said, "Well, lads, the Chief of Staff spoke to me this morning."

After the excitement had died down, a corporal said, "What did he say?"

"Well," said the driver, "he said, 'Tell me, Private Hoskins—when do you think this war is going to end?'"

HUNGRY MAN IN RESTAURANT: Waiter! There's a dead fly in my soup!
WAITER: Yes, sir, it's the heat that kills them.

Mary had a little lamb
And tied him to a heater.
And every time he turned around,
He burned his little seater.

The teacher was explaining to her second-year pupils how some materials will expand when hot and contract when cold.

"Can any of you," she asked, "think of anything else that does the same?"

"Sure," young Sally answered eagerly, "the days! In the summer, when it's hot, they get longer. And in winter, when it's cold, they get shorter."

IRATE NEIGHBOUR: I can hear your radio as if it were in my own flat!

NEIGHBOUR: Then will you help me make the monthly payments on it?

A ten-year-old boy stood patiently beside the clock counter one morning while the assistant waited on the adult customers. Finally he got around to the youngster, who made his purchase and hurried out to the curb, where his father was impatiently waiting in the car.

"What took you so long in there, Son?", he asked.

"The man waited on everybody in the shop before me," the boy replied. "But I got even," he added.

"How?"

"I wound all the alarm clocks while I was waiting," the youngster explained happily. "That's going to be a pretty noisy place at four o'clock today!"

"Is the doctor in?" inquired the caller.

"No, sir," answered his five-year-old son.

"Have you any idea when he will be back?"

"I don't know, sir—he went out on an eternity case."

WENDELL: What was your place like, at Blackpool?

RENDELL: Oh, OK—except that I kept getting disturbed in the mornings.

WENDELL: How come?

RENDELL: Well, at half-past six, the housekeeper got up to do the cleaning, and she woke me up. At seven o'clock the landlady got up to prepare the breakfasts, and that woke me up. At half-past seven, her husband got up to go to work, and *he* woke me up. At eight o'clock, their five children got up—and you know what *that* was like! . . . Then from eight o'clock on, it was quite peaceful.

WENDELL: Nobody else got up?

RENDELL: No. I had the bed to myself then.

•

Jimmie brought the following excuse to the teacher one morning.

"Please excuse Jimmie from being absent. He had a new baby brother. It was not his fault."

•

ADDLE: Where did Noah keep his bees?

PATE: In the archives (ark hives).

"O'Shea, your uncle is on the phone and he wants to know is your new baby a boy or a girl?"

"Well now, will you ask the poor silly man what else it *could* have been?"

JOKINGLY JOCULAR

● A reluctant soldier had just passed the medical for the army.

"But you can't take me," he protested, "I wear glasses."

"*That's* all right," said the medical officer kindly. "We'll put you right at the front so you won't miss anything."

• "Porter, the cook advises me that you were badly intoxicated last night and that you were trying to roll a barrel out of the basement. Can this be true?"

"Yes, my lord."

"And where was *I* during this performance?"

"In the barrel, my lord."

• PERRY: Why does the ocean roar?

TERRY: You would, too, if you had lobsters in your bed.

●

"Do you know why they didn't bury the Duke of Wellington with full military honours in 1850?"

"No—why?"

"He didn't die until 1852."

●

Do you know the difference between a bicycle and a sewing machine?

If you don't, you'd better be careful the next time you go to buy a bicycle, or they may sell you a sewing machine.

●

Sage Sam says that girls are all alike in that every one of them thinks she's different.

●

CORPULENT CUTHBERT: I'm disgusted.

FRIEND: Why?

CORPULENT CUTHBERT: I just stepped on a weighing machine and it said, "One person at a time."

●

EARNEST ERNEST: It says in the paper that they've caught the biggest hotel thief in Pricesea.

CYNICAL CLAUDE: Really? What hotel did he run?

After a very young and pretty secretary was hired, the office wolf lost no time in trying out his charms on her. He told her, with many flights of fancy, his miraculous feats on the football field, how many awards he had received, for his dancing, his bravery in the war—and anything else he could think of . . .

The girl grew weary and bored, so, after a particularly long and drawn-out account of some experience, she turned an innocent smile on him and asked, "Have you ever had a group photograph taken of yourself?"

The priest in a small Irish village was passing Mac's cottage on a Friday when he smelled something delicious. Looking in, he saw Mac frying a pan of sausages.

"Why, Mac," he said "What's this? Meat—

63

on a Friday! You must do a penance for this.

"You must bring a load of wood to the church."

Mac brought the load—but of sawdust.

"What's this?" said the priest, when he saw it. "I said a load of *wood*."

"Well," said Mac, "if sausages is meat, then sawdust is wood."

●

Broke Ben got a bill from one of his creditors. Written across the top in big red letters was: "This bill is one year old."

Ben sent it back, adding the message: "Happy Birthday."

●

DOUG: What did one tonsil say to the other tonsil?
PUG: The doctor is taking me out tonight.

KILLINGLY KUTE

Sour Sam, *about an old girlfriend who had just become engaged*: "Oh, they're just *perfect* for each other: he owns oil wells, and she's always gushing."

•

She was suspicious of his motives when, only two hours after meeting her on the beach, he declared that he loved her.

"I would like you to prove that you are capable of strong, faithful and everlasting love," she said.

"Well," he replied, "I can bring you dozens of references from other girls."

•

A stunning brunette, a new bride,
Went along in a bus for the ride.
  The conductor's "Your fare,"
  Was said with a glare.
"No, I'm not," she just grinned, "I've been dyed!"

•

"We were the best-drilled regiment in the army," said one old soldier to another. "Why, when we presented arms on parade, all you could hear was 'Slap-2-3-slap-2-3-slap'!"

"*We* were pretty good on drill, too," said his friend. "But of course we were mainly a fighting unit. When we presented arms, all you could hear was 'Slap-2-3-slap-2-3-slap-2-3-jingle'!"

"Jingle?" said the first old sweat. "What was that?"

"Medals!" said his friend.

66

• Salesgirl, *showing toy rocket to prospective customer*: "This is a very realistic space toy—half the time it doesn't work."

• Tramp, *at back door*: Ma'am *(whiningly)*, I haven't eaten for four days.

Plump Housewife: My! I wish I had your will power!

• Woman, *telephoning*: Doctor, I found your name in the phone book. Please come quickly. My husband's broken a leg!

Doctor: But I'm only a doctor of music.

Woman: Oh, *that's* OK—it's only the leg of the piano.

A city child visiting the country had just seen his first rainbow. With wonder and curiosity in his voice, he said to his mother, "It's very beautiful. What's it supposed to advertise?"

SALESLADY: Isn't this a pretty dolly? See—you put it to bed, it closes its eyes and goes right to sleep, just like a real baby. See?

LITTLE GIRL: I can see you don't know much about babies.

•

Mr. Marry's wife surprised him with triplets, and, when they all returned from the hospital, he had them all dressed up, put them into a splendid new perambulator, and sallied into town with them.

He met a friend who was taking his little boy for a walk. "Well," said Mr. Marry proudly to the little fellow, "what do you think of them?"

The little boy looked at the three little faces in the carriage, pointed to the biggest one and said, "Well, if I were you, I think I'd keep that one."

•

Elizabeth Taylor was coming out of the studio when she was accosted by a very tiny fan who asked for her autograph and added, "Do you mind printing your name? I can't read writing yet."

•

ARNY: If it took nine men nine hours to build a brick wall, how long would it take six men to build it?

BARNEY: None, because the nine men have already done the work.

Mother decided Betty had been attending school long enough to answer a few simple test questions. So she began with, "Tell me, dear, how long is a minute?"

"Which kind do you mean?" inquired the bright little girl, "A *real* minute—or a 'wait-a-minute'?"

ROMANTIC RENA: I met a gorgeous man on the beach today. He had a wonderful physique—especially at high tide.
FRIEND: What's high tide got to do with it?
ROMANTIC RENA: He was bow-legged.

FIRST DOG: My name is Fido. What's yours?
SECOND DOG: I'm not sure, but I think it's Down Boy.

It was little Benny's habit, on awakening in the morning, to climb out of his bed and crawl beneath the covers with his mother or his father.

But one day his parents got up early and left him sleeping peacefully in his bed. In a short while they heard piteous shrieks from overhead.

Dashing up to the bedroom, his mother flung open the door. The little fellow rushed to her arms, burst into tears and wailed, "Mother, I woke up and looked in your place, and you were not there. Then I looked in Daddy's place, and he wasn't there. And then I went back and looked in my place—and *I* wasn't there! Then I was afraid!"

Bettina, the little daughter of a tyre sales-man, had seen triplets for the first time.

"Oh, Mother," cried the little girl on returning home, "what do you think I saw today?"

"I can't imagine, dear—what?"

"A lady that had twins—and a spare!"

LOVE'S MOODS AND SENSES

Sally Salter, she was a young lady who taught,
And her friend Charley Church was a preacher who
    praught!
Though his enemies called him a screecher who
    scraught.

His heart when he saw her kept sinking and sunk,
And his eye, meeting hers, began winking and wunk;
While she in her turn fell to thinking, and thunk.

He hastened to woo her, and sweetly he wooed,
For his love grew until to a mountain it grewed,
And what he was longing to do then he doed.

In secret he wanted to speak—and he spoke—
To seek with his lips what his heart long had soke;
So he managed to let the truth leak, and it loke.

He asked her to ride to the church, and they rode,

They so sweetly did glide, that they both thought
    they glode,
And they came to the place to be tied, and were tode.

Then, "Homeward!" he said, "let us drive" and
    they drove,
And soon as they wished to arrive, they arrove;
For whatever *he* couldn't contrive *she* controve.

The kiss he was dying to steal, then he stole:
At the feet where he wanted to kneel, then he knole,
And said, "I feel better than ever I fole."

So they to each other kept clinging, and clung;
While time his swift circuit was winging, and wung;
And this was the thing he was bringing, and brung:

The man Sally wanted to catch, and had caught—
That she wanted from others to snatch—and had
    snaught—
Was the one that she now liked to scratch, and she
    scraught.

And Charley's warm love began freezing and froze,
While he took to teasing, and cruelly toze
The girl he had wished to be squeezing and squoze.

"Wretch!" he cried, when she threatened to leave
    him, and left,
"How could you deceive me, as you have deceft?"
And she answered, "I promised to cleave, and I've
    cleft!"

ANONYMOUS

74

LAUGHINGLY LUDICROUS

SAMMY: Mummy! the motor mower has just cut
off my foot!
MOTHER: Stay outside till it stops bleeding, dear:
I've just mopped the floor.

●

PATIENT, *on first visit to a psychiatrist*: Doctor, I have a very frightening delusion. I keep thinking there are *two* of me!

PSYCHIATRIST: Say that again, and *this* time, don't both speak at once!

●

MR. JESTER: I married a girl who was one of twins.

A FRIEND: How do you tell them apart?

MR. JESTER: Her brother has a beard.

A husband and wife decided to take their holidays separately for a change. The husband went to Blackpool and, two days later, his wife received this card from him: "The weather is here. Wish you were beautiful."

FATHER, *to his young son sitting on the kerb outside his house with a disconsolate expression on his face:* What's the matter, Bobby?

BOBBY: Well, if you must know—I just had an argument with your wife!

•

SILLY: What can you find in July but never find in
    August?
BILLY: The letter L.

•

CHLOE: How did mother find out that you didn't
    really take a bath?
JOEY: I forgot to wet the soap.

•

A man invented an ingenious machine for
cutting cabbage. His friends advised him to
exhibit it at the country agricultural show where
prizes were awarded for labour-saving gadgets that
would be of use in farm work.

On his return his friends gathered to meet
and congratulate him, for they had already heard
he had won a prize.

Sure enough, he was carrying a loving cup.

"That's terrific!" said a neighbour, slapping
him on the back. "What prize did you get?"

"Second prize," said the inventor.

"*Second*!" exclaimed the neighbour. "Why
didn't they give you *first* prize?"

"Well," said the inventor, "'twas like this:
the judges told me that, next to a knife, they had
never seen anything better for cutting cabbage."

78

The bride was crying most unhappily.

"What's the matter?" asked a visiting friend.

"Well," she replied, "I didn't find out until after our wedding that he's been married before and has six children."

"That *must* have come as a shock to you," her friend agreed.

"Yes," sobbed the bride. "And my own three children weren't pleased, either."

Three bishops on a camping trip were surprised to find, in their guide's cabin, that the stove was set in a most unusual position. It was set on posts about two metres above the cabin floor. They began to speculate as to the reason for this.

"Possibly the guide has found," the first one speculated, "that the heat radiating from the stove strikes the roof, this quickens the circulation, and the room is warmed in less time than if the stove were on the floor."

"No," the second one objected. "I am sure that the reason is that the green wood can be placed beneath it where the heat from the stove will dry it out, and hence it will burn better."

The third bishop thought that probably the stove was raised above the window so that cold, pure air could be had at night.

When the guide came, they asked him to settle the argument.

"Well," he explained, "when I brought that rig up the river, I lost some of the stovepipe overboard, and I had to set the stove up high so as to have enough pipe to reach through the roof!"

MONSTROUSLY MORONIC

IMPATIENT DINER: Are you the same waiter I gave my order to?

SLOW WAITER: Yes, sir.

IMPATIENT DINER: That's odd. I was expecting a much older man.

FUNNY PHIL thinks the story hilarious about the stingy baker who tried to save money by making the hole in his doughnuts bigger. He soon discovered that the bigger the hole the more dough it took to go around them!

Some recruits just never seem to catch on to Army routine, which isn't all that involved.

One such recruit was unusually slow in throwing himself into training, so the commanding officer sent for him.

"Tell me, what do you think of the Army?" he asked.

"I may learn to like it," the soldier replied, "but right now I think there's too much fussing around between meals."

Sam, the porter, was alone in the chemist's shop one evening when the 'phone rang. He answered with a confident "Hello."

"Hello," said the voice on the telephone. "This is Dr. Perry. Do you have tincture of trinitro-sulphate in aqueous solution?" he asked.

"Doctor," Sam said after a moment's pause, "when I said 'hello,' I told you all I know."

SMITH: I was in the regular army for seven and a half years.
JONES: Did you get a commission?
SMITH: No—just a straight salary.

MOTHER: Wouldn't you like to have a pretty cake with five candles on it for your party?

GREEDY GERTIE: I think I'd rather have five cakes and one candle, Mummy.

A Texas oilman dispatched an agent to buy some oil property. "Bid 32 million," he instructed, "but don't go over 34 million."

A couple of days later the agent was on the 'phone. "I got it for 33 million," he reported. "But we're in trouble."

"How come?" asked the boss.

"They want $5000 in cash!"

SILLY: Why did the moron sleep on the chandelier?

WILLY: Because he was a light sleeper.

Mr. Bucks, in a complaining voice: "My wife is always asking for money. Last week she wanted $100. The day before yesterday she asked me for $200. This morning she wanted $300."

"That's crazy," said his neighbour. "What does she *do* with it all?"

"*I* don't know, said Mr. Bucks. "I never give her any."

Not long ago a mother and her young son were shopping in a supermarket. The child, trying to be helpful, picked up a packet and brought it to her.

"Oh, no, dear," protested the mother. "Go and put it back. You have to cook that."

Mr. Smiley was absorbed in his favourite television programme when his son ventured to ask him about a homework problem.

"Dad," he asked, "where are the Alps?"

"Ask your mother," came the reply. "She puts everything away."

SAGE SAM: How can you always find a liar out?
SOLID SOLLY: Go to his house when he isn't in.

NICELY NUTTY

The cooks at the convent of Clonard,
Served eggs to their guests that were un-marred.
   They sang hymns as they toiled
   Until they were boiled.
Three verses for soft; ten for done-hard.

POLLY: Is it bad luck for a black cat to walk behind you?

MOLLY: That depends on whether you are a man or a mouse.

Sign in a busy New York drug store:
"*QUICK LUNCH, 75¢:* hamburger, coca cola, and one of our special all-purpose vitamin pills."

BONNIE: What did the beaver say to the tree.

JOHNNIE: It was nice gnawing you.

86

The man had been an international and champion jumper and now he suffered from pneumonia. The doctor came and took his temperature.

"How high?" asked the worried patient.

"One hundred and three and a bit," answered the medical man.

"What's the record?" came the anxious response.

●

"Now, Mr. Potter," said a temperance enthusiast to an election candidate, "I want to ask you a question. Do you ever take alcoholic drinks?"

"Before I answer the question," responded the suspicious candidate, "I want to know whether it is put as an inquiry or as an invitation!"

●

HUGHIE: Which insect is the most religious?
LOUIE:　A praying mantis.

●

MOPEY, *at summer camp, watching friend carry a small metal safe into his tent*: What's that for?
DOPEY: It's going to be my pillow.
MOPEY: Your *pillow*! Won't it be too hard?
DOPEY: What's the matter—you think I'm crazy? I'm going to stuff it with straw first.

A bather came out of the sea, shivering with cold, and ordered a hot coffee from a stand on the sands.

"Milk and sugar?" asked the counter-assistant.

"It doesn't matter," was the reply. "I'm going to pour it over my feet."

Money is the only thing that stands between most people and wealth.

"Goodbye," said the seaside landlady to a boarder as he prepared to leave. "And never darken my bath again!"

BESS: What goes well with orange, green, purple and yellow striped socks?
TESS: Hip boots.

Mrs. Newdriver was out driving and she noticed some linesmen working up on telegraph poles.

"What are they doing up there?" she asked her husband.

"Nothing," he said. "It's just that they heard you were coming."

AUNTIE: What did little Susie get at Penny's birthday party?
JANE: Three books, four handkerchiefs, and the measles.

The soldier serving in Hong Kong was annoyed and upset when his girl wrote breaking off their engagement and asking for her photograph back. He went out and collected from his friends all the unwanted photographs of women that he could find, bundled them all together and sent them back with a note saying, "Regret cannot remember which one is you—please keep your photo and return the others."

TEACHER: Can anyone tell me how trees become petrified?
EAGER STUDENT: The wind makes them rock.

CLEVER CARL: What do you call a thing which lies on the bottom of the sea and twitches?
BRIGHT BETTY: A nervous wreck.

ALVIN: What did the cat think when the dog caught him by the tail?
CALVIN: That's the end of me!

●

DOLEFUL DONALD: Did you hear about Uncle Robert?—He turned down the post of mortuary attendant!

SAD SARAH: Yeah. He musta thought it was a dead-end job.

●

CLEVER CLARA: How did the health inspector say good morning to his assistant?

BRIGHT BILLY: Hi, Jean.

●

GRUESOME GREGORY: Did you hear about the man who died from drinking varnish? It was an awful sight, but a beautiful finish.

●

Why do cows wear cowbells?

Because their horns don't honk.

●

What did one eye say to the other?

Just between you and me, there's something that smells.

POSITIVELY PUTRID

There was an old man of Kilbride,
Who slipped in a sewer and died.
  His stupid young brother,
  Went into another
And the verdict on both was "sewercide".

DOLEFUL DAN: Why did they put that great high
  fence around the graveyard?
GRUESOME GREG: Because so many people are dying
  to get in.

●

"I don't mind spending money to get knives sharpened," the seaside landlady told her new cook. "It's a lot cheaper than buying tender meat."

●

BLAKE: That hotel you recommended me to stay at in Southsea was terrible.

JAKE: Wasn't your room OK?

BLAKE: *Room!* It was like a telephone box with venetian blinds.

JAKE: The food was fresh, though, wasn't it?

BLAKE: I'll say it was. I had lobster one night, and I had to wrestle with it to see who would get the potatoes!

●

Which is the cleanest chemical in the lab?

Washing soda.

●

A man went to the rocket station and asked for a ticket to the moon.

"Sorry, sir," the attendant said, "the moon is full just now."

●

DOLEFUL DAN: Did you hear about the big fire at the shoe factory? Four thousand soles were lost.

QUALITY QUICKIES

• Why is it a mistake to gossip in a stable?

Because all horses carry tails.

• SANDY: Did you hear the story about the peacock?
MANDY: Yes, it's a beautiful tail.

DINER: Waiter! There's a fly in my soup!
WAITER: I know, sir, it's fly soup today.

What has four legs, a back, but no body?

A chair.

What does an elephant do when it rains?

It gets wet.

BILLY: Why is an empty matchbox superior to all
    others?
TILLY: Because it is matchless.

Why do lazy boys have to go to school?

The school won't come to them.

What do liars do when they die?

They lie still!

Why are ghosts like writing paper?

Because they appear in sheets.

How can you make a coat last?

Make the trousers and vest first.

What has four legs and feathers, and is neither animal nor bird?

A featherbed.

SILLY: What ball can't you play with?
BILLY: An eye ball.

MOLLY: Why is a good cabbage generous?
POLLY: Because it has a big heart.

Why are playing cards like wolves?

Because they come in a pack.

What can speak every language in the world?

An echo.

Do you know why Santa Claus planted a garden?

So he can "ho, ho, ho."

●

Doleful Donna says there won't be any witches this year—they're all on strike for electric brooms.

●

Smart: Why do we know that Robin Hood was an artist?
Alec: Because he was always drawing his bow.

●

Larry: What stands on one leg with its heart in its head?
Harry: A cabbage.

●

Celia: Why had Eve no fear of mumps?
Delia: Because she'd Adam!

ALVIN: Do you like bathing-beauties?
CALVIN: I don't know. I've never bathed one.

SMART: If you had sixteen cows and two goats, what
  would you have?
ALECK: Plenty of milk.

SMART SALLY says that baldness is the sign of a man
  who came out on top.

CORA: What musical instrument should never be believed?

DORA: A lyre.

PEARL: What is a good thing to lose?

SHIRL: A bad name.

SAGE SAM says that the best way to get a job done is to give it to a busy man . . . He'll have his secretary do it.

HARRY: What did one ear say to the other ear?

LARRY: Between you and me we need a haircut.

●

JENNY: What do cats strive for?
DENNY: Purrfection.

●

What can a whole apple do that a half apple can't?

It can look round.

RIOTOUSLY RUSTIC

●

"This seems just the ideal spot for a picnic," said Romantic Rena.

"I reckon it must be. Fifty million flies can't be wrong," replied Doleful Dan.

●

CITY BOY, *working on a farm for the summer, in a letter complaining to his dad:* It's like being an animal: you go to sleep with the chickens, get up with the rooster at dawn, work like a horse, eat like a pig, and get treated like a dog by the farmer.

AMATEUR FARMER: We milk our cow ten times a day.

VISITING NEIGHBOUR: That's crazy! Don't tell me she gives milk every time.

FARMER: Nope—but she's a good old Bossie—she do try hard each time.

●

BRAGGING FARMER: I've got hundreds and hundreds of cows.

CITY COUSIN: That's a lot of cows.

BRAGGING FARMER: Oh, yes! And I've got thousands of bulls, too.

CITY COUSIN: That's a lot of bull.

●

A farmer married a city girl, and in no time at all discovered she knew absolutely nothing about farm work. So he took her out to the barn to teach her how to milk the cows.

She was scared of them, though, and pleaded, "Aren't they big! Couldn't I just start on one of the calves?"

●

SUZY: Why should you never tell secrets in a cornfield?

WOOZY: Because corn has ears and is bound to be shocked.

On a walking holiday in Ireland a middle-aged couple found themselves at dusk one evening on a lonely road with no sign of the town where they were to spend the night. After some time they spied a man and woman rounding up their sheep, and asked them how far it was.

"Well, now, 'twould be a good three miles," the man said.

His wife, seeing the tourists' faces fall, whispered, "Ah, Paddy, make it two—sure, and they look so tired."

Young Robert was visiting in the country for the first time, and ran home excitedly, shouting, "Dad! Dad!, I've just seen a man who makes horses, and I watched him finish one."

"How do you know?" asked his dad.

"He was just nailing its back feet on," replied Robert.

CITY SLICKER: So you run a duck farm. Is business
   picking up?
FARMER: No. It's picking down.

●

"How do you like my cow?" asked the farmer
as he showed his stock to a young city visitor.

"She's nice—but isn't it a funny place she
has her fingers?"

●

"Oh—are you getting rid of that incubator,
Perkins?"

"Of course I am. I've had it six months, and
it hasn't laid an egg yet!"

●

An Australian sheep farmer, having received
a huge sum for his wool, bought a stunning Rolls
Royce Silver Cloud, lined with cream-coloured
suede, for an astronomical amount of money. When
he brought it back to the garage to have it serviced,
the salesman asked if he was thoroughly satisfied
with it.

"Oh, yes," said the farmer. "And I especially
like that glass partition you put between the front
seat and the back."

"Why?" the salesman asked.

"Because," said the farmer, "it will stop the
sheep from licking the back of my neck when I'm
taking them to market."

SOLIDLY STUPID

Saucy Susie went to the cinema in the afternoon. The man at the box office said, "Why aren't you in school?"

"Oh," replied Susie, "it's all right— I've got measles."

WIFE: Doctor, come quickly! My husband has swallowed his fountain pen.
DOCTOR: I'll be right over. What are you doing in the meantime?
WIFE: I'm using his pencil.

"I try to keep it quiet and orderly here," a fussy landlord told a prospective tenant. "Do you have children?"

"No," said the tenant.

"A piano, radio or phonograph?"

"No."

"Do you play any musical instrument, or have a dog, cat or parrot?"

"Nope," snapped the thoroughly annoyed tenant, "but my fountain pen scratches a little sometimes."

TEACHER: What are you painting?
LITTLE SAMMY: A cat.
TEACHER: Where's the tail?
LITTLE SAMMY: It's still in the paintbox.

108

Soldier's first letter home to his mother: "Dear Mum: you remember that I always used to love the army because the uniforms and the guns and the barracks were always kept so neat and clean and tidy? It's only since I joined up that I realized who it is that keeps them so neat and clean and tidy!"

●

At a military training camp, during the last war, each trainee was brought in before the assembled officers and asked what trade or branch of the service he would like to join. A gangling fellow with glasses came in.

"Now, my man," said the officer in charge, "what would *you* like to be?"

"A brigadier general," said the youth.

The officer exploded with anger. "Are you crazy?" he shouted.

"Sorry," said the youth. "I didn't know that was a necessary qualification."

The boss came down and found a boy in the stockroom just standing, leaning against a packing case. He asked, "How much are you getting a week?"

The boy answered, "Fifteen pounds."

"Here's your fifteen pounds. Now get out of here and don't come back!" the boss said angrily.

The boy put the money in his pocket and hurried out.

The boss then called to the stockroom manager and demanded, "How long has that fellow been working here?"

"He doesn't work here, he just delivered a parcel," answered the manager.

TEACHER: Tommy, where was the Declaration of
   Independence signed?
TOMMY: At the bottom, I guess.

GREEDY GRAHAM: I've eaten forty-nine eggs.
GULLIBLE GUS: Why didn't you eat one more and
   make it fifty?
GREEDY GRAHAM: Heh! do you want a man to make
   a pig of himself for just one egg?

Last summer, a mother looked out of her penthouse window down to the playground, where her two boys were having a splendid battle with their water pistols.

"Don't do that, boys!" she called. "Remember, water is scarce."

"Don't worry, mother," one of them shouted back. "We're not using water—we're using ink."

●

WILLY: What did the ice say when it started to melt?
NILLY: Oh dear! I feel a bit cracked.

●

Mrs. O'Rourke was puzzled.

"Why," she asked her friend, Mrs. O'Hara, "are the O'Briens learning French?"

"Don't you know? They've adopted a French baby and they want to be able to understand it when it starts talking."

●

NEW BRIDE: Darling, there is something I must tell you: before I met you, I was engaged to a boy with one leg called Horace.
NEW HUSBAND: You don't say! . . . What was his *other* leg called?"

BETTY: What, put in front of pies, will make them dangerous?
NETTIE: The letter S.

WELL: In what way can ten go into two?
BELLE: Yes—ten toes into two socks.

JESTER: What is a waste of time?
LESTER: Telling a hair-raising story to a bald-headed man.

Some paratroopers were aloft for their first jump, and everything went off in perfect order, until the last man came forward to jump.

"Hold it!" shouted his commanding officer. "You're not wearing your parachute!"

"Oh! that's all right, sir," retorted the recruit. "We're just practising today, aren't we?"

TOTALLY TATTY

A tramp was attacked by a dog with a threatening growl. The tramp attempted to pick up a stone to throw at him, but it was frozen fast.

"That's a great how-de-do!" said the tramp. "A fine country, this, where stones are tied down and dogs let loose!"

●

LAZY LUKE says, "You couldn't exactly say my wife
  has a really *big* mouth, but she's the only woman
  I know who eats a banana sideways.

●

BILLY: Have you heard the one about the bed?
MILLY: No, I haven't.
BILLY: No wonder—it hasn't been made up yet.

●

HIPPIE: How much are haircuts?
BARBER: Two dollars.
HIPPIE: Well, cut a dollar's worth off, please.

MOTHER: What in the world has happened to you? Your shirt is full of holes.

CHEEKY CHARLIE: We've been playing grocery store and I was the Swiss Cheese.

• • •

"Mummy," asked a little girl, "do men ever go to heaven?"

"Why, yes, of course, my dear," answered her mother. "Why do you ask?". .

"Because I've never seen angels with whiskers."

"Well," replied the mother, "some men do go to heaven, but they only get there by a close shave."

• • •

MIKE: My father runs a sea-side circus. We have a flea circus, too. My sister runs that. She's a very cooperative girl.

IKE: Cooperative? How?

MIKE: Oh, she's always itching to please.

UNIVERSALLY UNDERSTOOD

An elderly couple were sitting on deck-chairs on the beach, and the old man annoyed his wife by looking eagerly at every young girl who walked past.

"Anyone would think you'd never seen a pair of legs before," she muttered.

"That's just what I was thinking myself," mused the old man.

Some Broadway play producers were watching the star of an off-Broadway show.

"Wow! I wonder who made her dress," said one of them.

"It's hard to say," said the other. "Probably the police."

ROMANTIC RENA: My boy friend has been telling everybody he's going to marry the most beautiful girl in the world.

CATTY CATHIE: Oh, what a shame. And after all the time you two have been going together!

"Are caterpillars good to eat?" asked little Tommy at the dinner table.

"No," said his father, "what makes you ask a question like that while we are eating?"

"You had one on your lettuce, but it's gone now," replied Tommy.

PETER, *saying his prayers*: And please make Cyril give up throwing stones at me . . . By the way, I've mentioned this before.

●

"Well . . ." said the young graduate after the degree ceremony, "*that's* done. I went to college to please you and mother, you made such a fuss about it."

"Now," he said firmly, "I'm going to become a motorcycle cop just like I've been telling you from the time I was six years old!"

●

During a particularly fierce battle in North Africa in World War II, a private decided that discretion was the better part of valour, and set off for the rear. He had been travelling for several hours when a jeep came towards him along the road; it stopped alongside him and an officer stood up and shouted, "Hey, you, soldier—where do you think you're going?"

"There's a blooming great battle going on up there," said the private, "and I'm trying to get as far away from it as possible."

"Do you know who I am?" said the officer. "I am your commanding officer!"

"Blimey, I didn't realize I'd got as far to the rear as that!" said the soldier.

Two veterans were discussing a political boaster who usually campaigned strongly on the issue of his war record.

"The trouble with Hamblow," one observed, "is that he's always yelling about being ready to spill his last drop of blood—but he took mighty good care of the first drop."

"I dunno," said the second veteran. "In France, he was always where the bullets were thickest."

"Where was that?"

"In the munitions depot."

Little Georgie ran to his mother sobbing as though his heart would break.

"What's the matter, Georgie?" she asked.

"Daddy was hanging up a picture and he dropped it on his toe."

"Why, that's nothing to cry about; you should laugh at that."

"I did," sobbed Georgie.

Two girls were parading along the beach in their bikinis on the first day of their holidays.

"I want to find a man who doesn't drink, smoke, swear or philander," said one.

"What for?" asked her friend.

A lady who had been ill was advised by her doctor to spend a few weeks by the sea to recuperate. Her husband was unable to accompany her and, at a loss for something to do, she decided to use the time by keeping her eyes open for a young man for her rather plain unmarried daughter.

Lazing on the beach one day, she decided that the handsome young life-guard might be a likely prospect. Calling him over, she got straight to the point and said, "I'd like you to meet my daughter."

"What does she look like?" asked the young man.

"She's brainy and intelligent," was the reply.

"Yes, but is she good-looking?" he persisted.

"She's got a good job. She's a wonderful cook, and she makes all her own clothes."

"She sounds very nice, but is she pretty?"

"Her uncle died last year and left her £60,000, and . . ."

"Where is she? Where is she?"

SMART SUSIE: Which weighs more, a pound of feathers or a pound of lead?

SMARTER SAMANTHA: They weigh the same.

JOE: What's the best way to teach a girl to swim?

MOE: Well, you take her gently down to the water's edge, put your arm round her waist, and . . .

JOE: But, it's my sister.

MOE: Oh—just push her off the end of the pier.

●　A girl who had high hopes of becoming a concert pianist called one day on the pianist-composer Rubinstein to play for him. When the young woman had finished her number, she asked him, "What do you think I should do now?"

"Get married," said Rubinstein.

●

STERN PARENT: Christopher, I would like to go through one whole day without once scolding or punishing you.

CHRISTOPHER: Well, mother, you have my consent.

The doctor decided to put Mrs. Bulge on a diet.

"You can have three lettuce leaves," he said, "one piece of dry toast, a glass of orange juice and a tomato."

"Very well, Doctor," said Mrs. Bulge meekly. "Do I take them before or after meals?"

•

A bachelor, holidaying alone, was shown to his room by the landlady.

"The window's a bit small," he complained. "It wouldn't be much use in an emergency."

"There won't be an emergency," the landlady retorted. "My terms are cash in advance."

•

A tourist filling up his tank late at night at a Canadian service station noticed a puzzling smirk on the face of the attendant and asked him what the big joke was.

"You're the last person to be served with gas at the old price," was the reply.

The motorist had the pleasant feeling of finding a bargain. "You don't say," he said, smiling. "How come?"

"Well," the attendant replied, "tomorrow the price goes down eight cents a gallon."

A driver became so interested in talking to his friend that he missed the red light, and was halfway across a busy intersection when a police whistle brought him to his senses.

"Officer," he burbled, "I tried to stop—and I couldn't! I think there's something wrong with my car!"

"You're right, sonny," the cop said sarcastically. "I think it's the nut that holds the steering wheel!"

Chubby Charlie sat down at the lunch counter and ordered a whole pie.

"Shall I cut it into six pieces or eight?" asked the waitress.

"Six" said Charlie. "I'm on a diet."

VAIN VERA: Do you like my new bathing-suit? I got it for a ridiculous figure.
CATTY CATHY: You certainly did!

VARIOUSLY VACUOUS

• Sour Sue read her horoscope one day last week, and it told her "Make some new friends and see what happens."

She went out and made three new friends, and nothing happened.

Now she complains that she's stuck with three new friends!

•

To the editor of a small-town weekly newspaper, a letter saying:

Dear Sir:

Two weeks ago I lost a fine gold watch— one my grandfather gave to me when I was twenty-one. So right away I sent in an advertisement for your Lost and Found column.

Well—right after that, I went home and found that watch in the pocket of my Sunday suit. God bless your newspaper, sir!

● Paul and Polly got married in November, took a small apartment in New York, and invited their parents to share their first Thanksgiving dinner with them.

Thanksgiving afternoon arrived, the folks were not due till six o'clock, and Paul decided to go out and have a drink with the boys in order to keep out of his bride's way while she started to prepare the all-important meal.

"Not that you have too much to do," he told her, "I've plucked and stuffed the turkey. All you have to do is kill it and put it in the oven."

● LITTLE BOY: Baa, baa, black sheep, have you any wool?

BLACK SHEEP: What do you think *this* is—nylon?

●

TEACHER: Where is your pencil, Billy?

BILLY: I ain't got one.

TEACHER: Don't say *ain't* . . . Listen: *I* haven't a pencil. *You* haven't a pencil. *They* haven't a pencil.

BILLY: Gosh, where did all the pencils *go*?

●

A man asked the owner of a small travelling circus for a job and was offered that of lion tamer.

"It's really very easy," the owner explained. "The whole trick is simply to make the lions believe you're not afraid of them."

The man hesitated for a moment, and then said, "No, I don't think I could be that deceitful."

●

SUPERINTENDENT: Why do you *pull* that wheelbarrow, instead of *pushing* it, like you ought to?

WORKMAN: Well, guv'nor, I hates the sight of the bloomin' thing.

The teacher looked around the class. "Now," she asked brightly, "can anyone give me a connection between the animal and the vegetable kingdoms?"

Patrick put up his hand.

"Well, Patrick, what is it?"

"Please, Miss, Irish Stew, Miss."

Rob: What comes in without knocking?
Bob: The tide.

"Look," a man complained to the stationmaster. "I'm fed up with this waiting around. Can't you tell me the time the trains are supposed to run each day? Have you a time table?"

"*Time table*, is it? Bless your heart, it's a *calendar* we use here."

Mrs. Newdriver, *to her neighbour*: The only thing I don't like about parking is that noisy crash.

A middle-aged woman had inspected merchandise in every department in a big New York department store without spending a penny. Finally a tired salesman asked her, "Madam, are you shopping here?"

"Certainly," she replied, surprised. "What else do you think I'm doing?"

"Well, Madam," the salesman said in an acid tone, "I thought perhaps you were making an inventory."

At 2.30 a.m. a London man called a neighbour and said cherrily, "Gosh, isn't this a nice day?"

"Nice day!" exploded the neighbour. "Don't you know it's 2.30 and you got me out of bed?"

"Oh, that can't be true, for your dog is in my garden barking, and I can't believe you'd be letting him run loose at that time of night."

The dog hasn't been out at night since.

A worried-looking man in a big department store was approached by the floor manager.

"Looking for something in men's clothing, Sir?" he asked.

"No," came the reply, "something in woman's clothing—I've just lost my wife."

•

One day Abraham Lincoln was walking along a street in his home town with his two small sons, both of whom were crying lustily.

A neighbour stopped and inquired, "What's the matter with the boys?"

"Just the same as what's the matter with the whole world!" replied Lincoln. "I've got three walnuts and each of the boys wants two."

•

TEACHER: Alec, what month has 28 days in it?
SMART ALEC: They *all* do!

•

GREEK TAILOR, *examining trousers just brought in*: Euripides?
GREEK CUSTOMER: Yah, Eumenides.

•

When does it rain money?

Whenever there's some change in the weather.

•

WALLY: Why is tennis such a noisy game?
POLLY: Because each player raises a racket.

136

SMART: Why does a bald-headed man have no use for keys?

ALEX: Because he has lost his locks.

⬤

The Englishman on holiday at Southampton soon got bored with the company of a rich American who was staying at the same hotel, and was forever boasting about how much bigger and better everything was "back in the States."

Wondering how he could silence him as they walked together along the seafront, the Englishman saw the QE2 about a hundred yards from the shore. Quick as a flash, he leaned over the railings and shouted, "Come in Number Seven. Your time's up!"

⬤

"Mr. Smith," said the bank manager. "Your account is overdrawn by over £583."

"Let's be reasonable, and talk this over," said Smith. "I owe the bank £583 . . . But what was the state of my account three months ago?"

"Three months ago you were over £700 in credit."

"*So!*" said Smith, "Three months ago you owed *me* £700. And did *I* complain?"

"Does it ever rain here?" a holidaymaker asked a resident at a south coast resort.

"Rain?" the native repeated. "We've got five-year-old frogs in this town that haven't learned to swim yet."

●

"Is there any reason why the board should not recruit you into the army?"

"Yes, I have defective eyesight."

"Are you able to substantiate that claim?"

"Well—here's a photograph of my wife."

●

The marvellous part of a holiday by the sea is that it makes you feel good enough to return to work—and so poor that you have to.

"So sorry, conductor," the lady passenger on a train said apologetically, "but I'm afraid my little dog has eaten my ticket."

"Then I suggest, Madam," said the ticket-collector coolly, "that you buy him a second helping."

SMART SAM: Why does lightning shock people?
SMARTER SUZY: Because it doesn't know how to conduct itself.

●

The story is told about the Duke of Norfolk who, walking near his castle, was recognized by a villager. The latter commented on the ragged clothes the Duke was wearing as unsuitable for a man of his position in life.

"What difference does it make?" the Duke said. "I can wear any kind of clothes I wish to, because everybody here knows who I am."

A month later the same villager went to London, and in front of Claridge's he again saw the Duke—still wearing the same old togs, and again rebuked him.

"Oh, what difference does it make?" the Duke told him. "Here, nobody knows who I am."

●

MAMIE: What is it that you can lose and no one else can find for you?
JAMIE: Your temper.

●

A man stopped at a jeweller's to look at some watches that had been advertised in the local newspaper as selling below cost.

"If you're selling these below cost," he asked, "where does your profit come in?"

"Oh," replied the jeweller, "we make our profit repairing them."

Two friends were enjoying the meal and the host, O'Flaherty, couldn't resist boasting.

"Do you know I struggled an hour with that salmon?"

O'Ryan nodded.

"I know," he said sympathetically. "The tin-openers they make nowadays are no good at all."

The British don't care for the American habit of making tea with tea-bags. When a visitor to New York was asked how he liked his tea, he replied,

"Please, without surgical dressings!"

XPERTLY
XCELLENT

It was evident the new member of the club was new to the game of golf, for he took swipe after swipe at the ball without touching it.

Finally, though, something flew forward in front of him and he straightened up with a happy sigh of satisfaction.

"Thank goodness!" he exclaimed. "It's gone at last!"

"Excuse me, sir," said the caddy, "but that was your wristwatch."

A little boy was crying on the beach, "Ooh— I can't find my mummy. I'm lost!"

As he wailed his way along the beach sympathetic bathers gave him pennies and chocolate.

After about a half hour a woman ran after him crying, "I know where your mummy is, little boy."

"So do I!" he hissed. "Shut up and go away!"

DANGEROUS DAN: My first job was as a human cannonball.

AWED FRIEND: Did you get much money?

DANGEROUS DAN: No—only travelling expenses.

BRILLIANT BILLY: Which mythological character has a very good drainage system?
CLEVER KATE: Pan—he had pipes.

●

FATHER: Peter, why do bells ring at Christmas?
PETER: Because someone is pulling the rope.

●

RICH TEXAN, *dictating his will to his lawyer*: To my son I leave five million dollars—and he's lucky I didn't cut him out of my will entirely!

●

They were giving away balloons at a local shop and the place was crowded with children, all anxious to receive one of the playthings. As one small boy came up to the assistant, he asked politely if he might have two balloons.

"I'm sorry," was the reply, "but we only give one balloon to each boy. Have you a brother at home?"

The youngster was truthful, but he did want another balloon.

"No," he said, "but my sister has, and I want one for him."

A man brought before the Judge because of a huge debt for which he was being sued cried out to the judge, "As God is my judge, I do not owe this money!"

The Judge replied, "He's not, I am, you do."

YAKKETTY-YAK

•

"O'Shea, how is it that whenever you ask an Irishman a question, he always answers with another?"

"Who told you *that* nonsense?"

POLITICIAN: Did your paper say I was a liar and a scoundrel?

EDITOR: It did not.

POLITICIAN: Well, *some* paper in this town said so.

EDITOR: It may have been that other newspaper down the street. We never print stale news.

Mrs. Manychildren's friends are surprised by how often they have come into her house to find her listening to music on the radio—or even just talks—in foreign languages. One of them asked her why.

"Well," she said, "our George sings and plays a guitar; Sally has a banjo; Paul brings the college group he sings with home sometimes during the holidays . . . It's just that, after listening to all those modern lyrics it's a *joy* to listen to something and not know what they're saying!"

The zoo giraffe died, and its keeper sat beside the corpse, weeping loudly.

"There, there, now," said a motherly-looking visitor. "Try to bear up under this sorrow. I know it must be a terrible shock and sadness to you, after all the years you have taken such good care of this animal so dear to you, but . . . ."

147

"*Dear* to me," the man interrupted. "Dear nothing! It's my job to *bury* the darn thing!"

●

BOASTFUL BOB, *telling a story*: On my right hand was a lion, on my left was a tiger, in front and at the back of me were wild elephants.
GULLIBLE GUS: What happened?
BOASTFUL BOB: The merry-go-round stopped.

●

Two small girls were comparing their mothers, who were both active club members.

"My mother can talk on just about any subject," Pattie declared proudly.

"Ah," replied Hattie, "my mother can talk without any subject at all."

●

Two holidaymakers met on the promenade and struck up a friendship.

"Does your hotel overlook the sea?" asked one.

"Yes," said the other. "And it overlooks comfortable beds, good food and just about everything else!"

●

JERRY: What is the longest word in the English language?
TERRY: Smiles, because there is a mile between its first and last letter.

●

THE BLIND MEN AND THE ELEPHANT

It was six men of Indostan
To learning much inclined,
Who went to see the elephant
(Though all of them were blind)
That each by observation
Might satisfy his mind.

The first approached the elephant,
And, happening to fall
Against his broad and sturdy side,
At once began to bawl,
"God bless me! but the elephant
Is very like a wall!"

The second, feeling of the tusk,
Cried: "Ho! what have we here,
So very round and sharp?
To me 'tis mighty clear—
This wonder of an elephant
Is very like a spear!"

The third approached the animal,
And, happening to take
The squirming trunk within his hands,
Thus boldly up and spake:
"I see," quoth he, "the elephant
Is very like a snake!"

The fourth reached out his eager hand,
And felt about the knee;
"What most this wondrous beast is like
Is mighty plain," quoth he;
"'Tis clear enough the elephant
Is very like a tree."

The fifth, who chanced to touch the ear,
Said: "E'en the blindest man
Can tell what this resembles most.
Deny the fact who can:
This marvel of an elephant
Is very like a fan!"

The sixth no sooner had begun
About the beast to grope,
Than, seizing on the swinging tail
That fell within his scope,
"I see," quoth he, "the elephant
Is very like a rope!"

And so these men of Indostan
Disputed loud and long,
Each in his own opinion
Exceeding stiff and strong,
Though each was partly in the right,
And all were in the wrong!

So, oft in theologic wars
The disputants, I ween,
Rail on in utter ignorance
Of what each other mean,
And prate about an elephant
Not one of them has seen!

JOHN GODFREY SAXE

ZESTFULLY ZANY

•

An important Turkish Embassy official managed to wangle an audience with the Sultan.

The Sultan looked at him searchingly, then said pleasantly, "I don't recall your name, but the fez is familiar."

Ad in local paper: Wanted: female cat for light mouse-keeping.

A very pretty, very bitter and very, very angry girl was bent on revenge. So she wrapped her diamond engagement ring carefully in cotton and tissue paper, tucked it into a box, and addressed it to her former fiancé.

Then she pasted a label in a prominent place, upon which was inscribed in large red letters, "Glass—Handle with Care."

MAN (*at the seaside*): Madam, is that your boy who is burying my coat in the sand?

MOTHER: No, that's my friend's little boy. Mine is the one sailing your hat in the sea.

154

THE WONDERFUL "ONE-HOSS SHAY"

Have you heard of the wonderful one-hoss shay,
That was built in such a logical way
It ran a hundred years to a day,
And then, of a sudden, it—ah, but stay,
I'll tell you what happened without delay,
Scaring the parson into fits,
Frightening people out of their wits, —
Have you ever heard of that, I say?

Seventeen hundred and fifty-five.
Georgius Secundus was then alive, —
Snuffy old drone from the German hive.
That was the year when Lisbon-town
Saw the earth open and gulp her down,
And Braddock's army was done so brown,
Left without a scalp to its crown.
It was on the terrible Earthquake-day
That the Deacon finished the one-hoss shay.

Now in building of chaises, I tell you what,
There is always *somewhere* a weakest spot, —
In hub, tire, felloe, in spring or thill,
In panel, or crossbar, or floor, or sill,
In screw, bolt, thoroughbrace,—lurking still,
Find it somewhere you must and will,—
Above or below, or within or without, —
And that's the reason, beyond a doubt,
That a chaise *breaks down*, but doesn't *wear out.*

But the Deacon swore (as Deacons do,
With an "I dew vum," or an "I tell *yeou*,")
He "would build one shay to beat the taown
'N' the keounty 'n' all the kentry raoun';
It should be so built that it *couldn't* break daown:"
—"Fur," said the Deacon, "'t's mighty plain
Thut the weakes' place mus' stan' the strain;
'N' the way t' fix it, uz I maintain,
Is only jest
T' make that place uz strong uz the rest."

So the Deacon inquired of the village folk
Where he could find the strongest oak,
That couldn't be split nor bent nor broke, —
That was for spokes and floor and sills;
He sent for lancewood to make the thills;
The crossbars were ash, from the straightest trees,
The panels of white-wood, that cuts like cheese,

But lasts like iron for things like these;
The hubs of logs from the "Settler's Ellum," —
Last of its timber,—they couldn't sell 'em,
Never an axe had seen their chips,
And the wedges flew from between their lips,
Their blunt ends frizzled like celery-tips;
Step and prop-iron, bolt and screw,
Spring, tire, axle, and linchpin, too,
Steel of the finest, bright and blue;
Thoroughbrace bison-skin, thick and wide.

Boot, top, dasher, from tough old hide
Found in the pit when the tanner died.
That was the way he "put her through." —
"There!" said the Deacon, "naow she'll dew!"

Do! I tell you, I rather guess
She was a wonder, and nothing less!
Colts grew horses, beards turned gray,
Deacon and Deaconess dropped away,
Children and grandchildren—where were they?
But there stood the stout old one-hoss shay
As fresh as on Lisbon Earthquake-day!
Eighteen hundred;—it came and found
The Deacon's masterpiece strong and sound.
Eighteen hundred increased by ten; —
"Hahnsum kerridge" they called it then.
Eighteen hundred and twenty came; —
Running as usual; much the same.

Thirty and forty at last arrive,
And then come fifty, and fifty-five.

Little of all we value here
Wakes on the morn of its hundredth year
Without both feeling and looking queer.
In fact, there's nothing that keeps its youth,
So far as I know, but a tree and truth.
(This is a moral that runs at large;
Take it.—You're welcome.—No extra charge.)
First of November,—the Earthquake-day—
There are traces of age in the one-hoss shay,
A general flavour of mild decay,
But nothing local, as one may say,
There couldn't be,—for the Deacon's art
Had made it so like in every part
That there wasn't a chance for one to start.
For the wheels were just as strong as the thills,
And the floor was just as strong as the sills,
And the panels just as strong as the floor,
And the whiffle-tree neither less nor more,
And the back crossbar as strong as the fore,
And spring and axle and hub *encore*.
And yet, *as a whole*, it is past a doubt
In another hour it will be *worn out*!

OLIVER WENDELL HOLMES